Water, bread and wine

Water, bread and wine

The New Testament
view of the relationship between
baptism and the Lord's supper

Peter Naylor

Grace Publications

GRACE PUBLICATIONS TRUST

General Editors
John Appleby
Peter M. Misselbrook, M.A., B.D.

Grace Publications Trust
139 Grosvenor Avenue
London N5 2NH

© Peter Naylor, M. Th. 1989

ISBN 0 946462 17 8

Distributed by:
EVANGELICAL PRESS
12 Wooler Street, Darlington, Co Durham DL1 1RQ,
England

Cover design by
Mrs. J. C. Davison

Printed in Great Britain by Cox and Wyman, Reading

Contents

Preface

A book of puzzles which I have seen contained the following teaser:

Find three empty beakers and three knives (not sharp). Place the beakers upside down on the ground in the form of a triangle with equal sides, each side being a little longer than any one of the knives. Then make a platform with the knives on top of the beakers in such a way that no part of any knife touches the ground. The finished platform has to be strong enough to bear a fourth beaker filled with water.

Try it!

This booklet examines the place of communion in New Testament churchmanship, and therefore in contemporary church life.

1.
Beginnings

In Acts 2 we read the apostle Peter's famous sermon to the people of Jerusalem fifty days after the resurrection of Jesus. Addressing many who shared responsibility for the suffering of the Lord, he urged them to confess their faults, seek the mercy of God and acknowledge Jesus as the Christ. The fact that Jesus had left the company of the dead and had ascended into heaven itself showed, Peter claimed, that they had erred grievously: the people had been in conflict with one who had shown himself to be the holy Son of God. Peter then asserted that the reality of Jesus' glorification had been proven in two ways: first, his disciples had actually seen him in his risen state; second, the evident presence of the Holy Spirit among his followers on the Day of Pentecost was a fulfilment of ancient predictions concerning the sufferings and the triumph of the Messiah.

Peter's words had a salutary effect on his hearers. They were 'cut to the heart' (Acts 2:37). They realised the enormity of what they had done. They saw that Jesus was none other than the long-expected Christ and that he whom they had rejected would ultimately hold them to account. Their hearts were pierced by guilt. They had never been so miserable or had felt so sinful. In short, they did not know until then what it was to fear God. They realized that the strange phenomena which they had witnessed among the disciples of Jesus demonstrated that the Almighty was very near them. Understandably, therefore, they put a question to Peter and his colleagues: 'What shall we do?' They knew that they needed help, and they sought it from those who had correctly assessed their faults. The immediate reply from the apostle was: 'Repent, and let every one of you be baptized in the name of Jesus Christ for the remission of sins' (Acts 2:38). In these words a confident Peter presented Jesus as the Christ who must be confessed as such by the people if they desired to be saved. To rescue themselves from the wrath of God and from a doomed society they must be washed in the Name of Jesus the Messiah. The record states that about three thousand of them were obedient (Acts 2:41).

The same chapter tells us that an amazing and irreversible change came over this company. Judging by what is written in Acts 2:41-47 they actually became changed people. They not only listened to Peter's words and received baptism, but they afterwards followed the apostles and were found continually in their company, showing a desire to learn all that they could about Jesus from those who had been with him. Almost as a matter of course they opened up their homes and ate together. Financial and material burdens were shared as they learned the joy of giving to others. They were an obviously happy company of people whereas, when listening to Peter's sermon, they had been in a state of deep dejection. Now they displayed a singular humility towards each other and found favour with God and men, drawing people to themselves.

Above all else, their religion had been transformed. They were 'praising God' together (Acts 2:47). Obviously, something very fundamental had happened: Peter's conditional promise in verse 38, 'you shall receive the gift of the Holy Spirit', had been fulfilled.

These events at Jerusalem following the Day of Pentecost were only a beginning. The book of Acts and the Epistles display the gospel of the grace of God turning a sinful world upside down.

The Word of God has been proclaimed continuously since the age of the apostles. Men and women in every time and land have gladly received it. The church of Jesus Christ has marched on. It has frequently suffered for its faith. It has often been injured from within by those who have been unfaithful to its Scriptures Nevertheless, it has always included believers who have shared together in faith and worship, enjoying and proclaiming the love of God in Jesus Christ.

2.
Where is the church?

The Last Supper was the very first communion meal (Matthew 26:17-29, cf. parallel references in the other Gospels and 1 Corinthians 11:23-25). Since New Testament times Christian people have always gathered together in their churches to eat and drink in memory of their Saviour. But what is really meant by 'church'? To answer this question it is necessary to examine the way in which this and other words are used in both the Old and New Testaments. This wide subject relates to many other Biblical doctrines; here, the 'church' is considered solely in its role as a means for fellowship between believers.

The meaning of 'church'

The words 'congregation' or 'assembly' are often employed in the Old Testament, being equivalent to 'church' in the New Testament. An assembly was a body of people gathered together for a particular purpose. It involved the one who called, those who were called and an agenda or programme for the meeting. The people concerned were deliberately summoned: they never gathered spontaneously. When they were together, the summoning authority would present them with matters of common concern. For example, Moses reminded Israel about 'the day you stood before the Lord your God in Horeb, when the Lord said to me, "Gather the people to me, and I will let them hear my words" ' (Deuteronomy 4:10). It would not be inaccurate to render this 'make the people into a church, and I will make them hear my words'.

This meaning carries over into the New Testament where the words 'church' and 'assembly' are usually (though not invariably) employed with reference to Christian people. An interesting exception to this is found in Acts 19:32 and 39. The context mentions a large and somewhat uncontrolled crowd in the city of Ephesus brought together at the instigation of the silversmith Demetrius and his pagan colleagues. The townspeople met in one place and for a particular purpose, even though many did not really know what it was all about! Nevertheless, they constituted an 'assembly' or 'church'.

One church

The Ephesian incident helps to illustrate a basic New Testament truth concerning the growth of the kingdom of heaven. This kingdom includes all those who are summoned by God to hear and serve him and who are constituted by him as a 'church'. Because there is only one kingdom it follows that there is only one church, a doctrine emphasized finely by Ephesians 4:4-6. Here the apostle Paul writes about the one assembly of Jesus Christ within which there is one Spirit, one hope, one Lord, one faith, one standard pattern of baptism and one heavenly Father. Christian believers are said to belong to this one church of God which, by definition, embraces all the saints of all times. In the same letter (5:23-32) Paul gives especially rich expression to this concept, repeatedly describing the church of God as a body which includes all believers. The word 'church' occurs no less than six times in this context because the apostle intends to be emphatic about the essential oneness of the people of God: the Lord has just the one assembly.

Many churches

Yet the New Testament is entirely practical. It shows that the one church is divided into small working cells or units. Each bears the name given to the total fellowship; each is a 'church'. This is extremely important. The logical inference is that because the one church is composed of 'churches', that which characterizes the whole is a feature of each part: the church universal is mirrored and represented by the locally-gathered church, the latter being a miniature model of the whole assembly.

The New Testament accepts that because there is so much which inevitably separates the Lord's people from each other (for example, death, time and distance), some form of organization is required to keep believers in fellowship together. The stated unit of organization is the local church. The New Testament teaches that each gathered fellowship of Christians, governed by its Head, the Lord Jesus Christ, possesses sufficient means to pursue its calling. Although Scripture has much to say about the universal church, its practical emphasis falls upon locally-gathered churches, groups of believers called together by the Holy Spirit in which the Lord's people worship and find their fellowship in service together.

In the Gospel of Matthew, Christ speaks about the whole church as militant and evangelical; it will boldly attack the citadel of hell and batter down its gates (16:18). Yet, when speaking about practical Christian conduct, the Lord assumes that his disciples will one day be members of local fellowships. He describes the 'church' (18:17) as a coherent and visible body of believing people to whom the individual member may come with his personal problems.

Some examples of local churches

The book of Acts describes the establishment of several such churches, recording that when the gospel was preached indiscriminately to all men some turned to Christ and, as disciples, gathered together spontaneously to worship God. Furthermore, their 'togetherness' developed to the point of organization: they formed identifiable 'churches' led by elders and subscribing to apostolic teaching. Although they always related to each other in practical ways, these churches were separate entities.

The earliest and most outstanding example is the church at Jerusalem, *which came into being with the three thousand who were converted and baptized on the Day of Pentecost.* These disciples stayed together with the apostles and maintained what was, in all essentials, the normal life of a Christian church (Acts 2:42 onwards). Their setting-apart of men to care for material matters (6:5) was typical in this respect. While the appointment of such men was suggested by the apostles, it was actually made by the larger fellowship of believers. This fellowship was effectively a 'church', with a corporate mind

and will of its own. Acts 8:1 actually describes this assembly
as a church, as do 11:22 and 15:22. There had come into being
within Jerusalem an identifiable communion, separate from
the Jewish public, eventually to be in fellowship with Christians elsewhere but with its own internal life and pattern of
ministry.

Another example is the church at Antioch. Acts 11:19-21
relates that the gospel was preached to both Jews and Greeks
in that city. Many people turned to Christ. The growth of the
work at Antioch was so rapid that the church in Jerusalem took
an active interest in what was happening (11:22) and sent
Barnabas to inquire. He stayed there with his colleague Saul
for at least a year. During that time the believers at Antioch
showed such a zeal for their faith that they attracted to
themselves the nickname 'Christian'. A little later on, this
church possessed prophets and teachers (13:1) and was even
guided by the Lord himself to initiate the first-ever missionary
enterprise: it was the Antioch church which sent Barnabas and
Saul away to Cyprus to preach the gospel. A Christian cell
endeavoured to reproduce itself.

Two churches had now emerged: those at Jerusalem and
Antioch. Although separate in identity, they were obviously
expressions of the one church of Christ. Furthermore, Jerusalem had taken an interest in Antioch and Antioch had sought
to establish new churches elsewhere. In all this activity the
Head of the Church was obviously concerning himself with
the establishment of living groups of believers who were
anxious to help one another and to reproduce their fellowships
in ever-widening circles.

During his second missionary journey Paul came to the
vast community of Corinth and preached the gospel there
(Acts 18:8). As a result, many were converted and baptized.
The apostle stayed in the city for a year and a half to give

systematic teaching to the new believers. In later years he wrote letters to the fellowship, which he called 'the church of God which is at Corinth' (1 Corinthians 1:2). Yet he never thought of Corinth as the only church: he knew that there were others. The same verse also addresses 'all who in every place call on the name of Jesus Christ our Lord'.

The church at Ephesus is another prominent example. Paul's first visit to this city is recorded in Acts 18:19. He did not stay long on this occasion, but when he returned (19:1) he remained there for some two years (19:10). Many Jews and Greeks were converted under his ministry and an organized church grew up. Paul's last visit is recorded in 20:17-38. He called 'the elders of the church' (verse 17). Later, he wrote to that same fellowship, which he evidently considered to be a properly-constituted assembly. Its separate identity as a church was subsequently acknowledged by the Saviour himself in very direct fashion by his threat to close it down (Revelation 2:5).

There are many other examples. Acts 14:23 speaks about Paul and his colleagues ordaining 'elders in every church'. Part of the apostle's task in his second missionary journey was to travel round 'strengthening the churches' (Acts 15:41). Because of his activities the churches were 'strengthened in the faith, and increased in numbers daily' (Acts 16:5). Romans 16:4 refers to the 'churches of the Gentiles' and Galatians 1:22 to fellowships which were predominantly Jewish. Writing to the Corinthians, Paul alludes to their practice of receiving letters of commendation from visiting Christians before such friends were admitted to the fellowship of the host church (2 Corinthians 3:1). Much within the 'pastoral' letters reflects the ministries of Timothy and Titus in local settings. The letter of Paul to Philemon and that from John to Gaius presume local self-governing and self-supporting fellowships.

Although the book of the Revelation was sent by God the Father through his Son to all his servants, it was addressed in the first instance to the 'seven churches which are in Asia' (1:4). Throughout the New Testament the church of Jesus is considered as cellular, the individual churches being the cells.

The sufficiency of the local church

As this cellular concept would suggest, there is nothing that Christian people do or that the church of Christ undertakes which should ever be separated from the basic context of the local fellowship. The Scriptures dislike what could be termed 'individualism': the Lord's people are exhorted to act within and on behalf of their churches (Hebrews 10:25, 13:17). On the other hand, the New Testament does not contemplate any action group larger than the gathered church. It is true that various assemblies did *sometimes* join resources for the purposes of discussion, giving or missionary enterprise (Acts 11:29, 15:1-35, Romans 15:26-28); but their co-operation was by mutual consent and was never intended to consolidate any lasting form of inter-church organization. So bishops or elders were invariably servants within their own fellowship. This is brought out, for example, in Titus 1:5: 'For this reason I left you in Crete, that you should ... appoint the elders in every city.' Apart from the *apostles and their representatives, leaders did not guide in churches other than their own;* episcopacy was never extramural.

In short, every characteristic of the whole Christian church may be observed within the individual churches. All the New Testament churches appeared as microcosms of the whole. Each communion is presented as a living cell, sufficient in itself and within which there was structure and control.

Although relationships between various churches were sometimes very strong they never involved any permanent system of administration. While the New Testament makes it clear that the churches were always required to strengthen their mutual bonds of fellowship it says absolutely nothing about any form of inter-church government. Not even the apostles attempted to develop external, centralized control. Although Paul sought to impose his teaching upon all the churches he assumed that they possessed an equality of status; the apostle never gave any particular church a position of seniority among the others.

The ordinances of the church

The two ordinances of the Lord Jesus Christ, baptism and the communion meal, were administered within the context of local churches where such existed. Converts who were baptized in areas where there were no pre-existing fellowships immediately formed their own wherever they could, as at Jerusalem on the Day of Pentecost. For this reason the Lord's supper is presented as a regular expression of local fellowship. Even if there was no relevant information from the New Testament letters about this, reason would conclude that communion was meant as an opportunity for the members of a gathered church to share worship together. From the Gospels alone it might be supposed that the more developed teaching of the New Testament would present communion as an exclusive meal to which unbelievers and even interested but unbaptized and presumably uncommitted friends would not be welcomed. (This conclusion, of course, would assume that baptism was mandatory for all who had become disciples before the resurrection as well as for converts after Pentecost.)

It might further be supposed that visitors would only be given a place upon production of satisfactory evidence demonstrating that they believed and had been baptized.

Such presuppositions are in fact borne out entirely by Paul's correspondence with the Corinthian church. 1 Corinthians expands and applies basic information supplied by the Gospels, presenting communion as a glorious expression of local church life.

3.
Obedience

As soon as the good news began to be proclaimed to non-Jews there arose the question of whether foreign converts should be circumcised, that is, become Jewish themselves. To many Jews it seemed well-nigh incredible that the God of their fathers should not require strict obedience to the laws of Moses from all Gentile believers. It was obvious that God was calling Asians, Greeks and others to himself. Beyond doubt many foreigners were turning to the Messiah of Israel in their own homelands. Surely, these uncircumcised believers would have to enter the fold of the ancient church? The oracles of God had come to Israel (Romans 3:2), while the Messiah himself was of the seed of David (Romans 1:3). The apostles were all Jews, and after Pentecost believers had met within the precincts of the temple of God at Jerusalem (Acts 5:12). Other peoples, it was felt, would be more than welcome to enter the fellowship of the Messianic community so long as they identified themselves with the Messiah's race by giving full allegiance to Moses. In other words they had to become Jews.

Acts 15:1 says that 'certain men came down from Judea (to Antioch) and taught the brethren, "Unless you are circumcised according to the custom of Moses, you cannot be saved."'

The first Christian council

This unhappy intrusion into the life of the rapidly multiplying churches was nothing less than a carefully orchestrated attempt to impose the whole body of Mosaic law upon all Christian disciples. In effect, the problem within the fellowship at Antioch became a crucial test case: here Gentiles were the first to be required to give obedience to the complete spectrum of Jewish legal and ritual observance as interpreted by Pharisaism.

Had this view prevailed at Antioch it would have carried the day everywhere else. Christianity, had it continued at all, would have been merely an emphasis within traditional Judaism and therefore emptied of all meaning. The apostles knew this. Yet, given the Jewish background of most of the first converts, it seemed plausible enough to many. Nevertheless, the council of apostles and elders which discussed the issue at Jerusalem (Acts 15:2-29) saw the matter quite differently. Peter asked the company, 'Why do you test God by putting a yoke on the neck of the disciples which neither our fathers nor we were able to bear? But we believe that through the grace of the Lord Jesus Christ we shall be saved in the same manner as they' (15:10-11). He believed that certain vital truths were under attack in this controversy and that they would be denied if Pharisaism had its way.

The apostles and elders at Jerusalem decided that Gentile converts would never be required to become Jews. They were already saved by faith in Christ and could receive no benefit whatever from circumcision and Jewish ritual. On the contrary, traditional Judaism would only blind their eyes to the great truths of the gospel. The council was not slow to assert that its verdict came from the mind of God himself (Acts 15:28) and refused flatly to impose Judaism upon Gentile converts. Its decree says nothing about fast days, feast days, tithing, sabbath observance or any other Jewish distinctives with the sole exception of a prohibition against the consumption of blood, this being undoubtedly a concession to Jewish sensitivity.

New Testament formalities

Nevertheless, the Christian churches were not without certain outward forms for their worship. In particular, Christ himself had taken two Jewish observances to adapt them for use by his followers: ritual washing and the Passover meal became the precedents for the ordinances of baptism and communion.

Ablutions had been a prominent feature within the laws of Moses (for example, the cleansing of the leper, Leviticus 14) and had been an integral part of the ministry of John the Baptist at the river Jordan. Like John, Christ made water baptism mandatory for all disciples both before and after Pentecost (John 3:22, 4:1; Matthew 28:19).

Concerning the communion table, it is obvious from the Gospel records that the Last Supper was a Passover. Transformed by our Lord, it developed into a regular fellowship meal. Apart from baptism, it was the only formal procedure which the churches received from Christ involving material aids.

The prominent absence of Jewish observances in the churches puts into exceptionally bold relief the Lord's commands to baptize converts who should then gather with other believers at his table. Just as Moses' laws were considered as binding on all Jews (and remember, the Lord and the apostles never denied this), so Christ's two ordinances were no less binding for all Christian believers. The worship of Israel in Old Testament times relied heavily upon the employment of visual forms in an exposition and anticipation of the Messianic dispensation to come. This dispensation, when it arrived, involved a drastic reduction in the use of such visual forms. Nevertheless, forms were not totally eliminated: a degree of what could even be described as 'ceremonial' was deliberately maintained. While Old Testament rites looked forward, new covenant ordinances look back as well as to the end. Baptism is simultaneously a declaration of personal faith in the Saviour who has come and a portrayal of the cleansing which Christ gives to the believer. The Lord's supper is a memorial of the death of Christ. In the same way that many outward forms had been compulsory in national Israel, a few outward forms became just as compulsory in the new, international Israel.

Baptism

The New Testament refers to the earliest disciples as those who were to baptize others, Matthew 28:19 including the instruction to 'go ... baptizing'. In other words, Scripture sees baptism as an instrument to be applied by the evangelist when helping a new convert. It becomes part of the convert's total experience of conversion. Undoubtedly this is why the Lord explained carefully to the apostles whom they should baptize.

Baptized themselves, the apostles would baptize all new converts without exception as part of their general ministry.

The book of Acts shows clearly that they did this. When Peter was asked by his trembling hearers on the Day of Pentecost what they should do to save themselves from their sins, he thundered the message that they ought to 'repent, and let everyone of you be baptized in the name of Jesus Christ' (Acts 2:38). The remainder of the New Testament is no less dogmatic.

If the logic of this position were to be applied nowadays it would follow that churches which fail to baptize all believers upon profession of faith before receiving them into communicant fellowship are not completely loyal to the word of God.

Communion

Luke 22:19-20 provides one account of the institution of the Lord's supper: 'and he took bread, gave thanks and broke it, and gave it to them, saying, "This is my body which is given for you, do this in remembrance of me." Likewise he also took the cup after supper, saying, "This cup is the new covenant in my blood, which is shed for you." ' The word 'do' is a command, Jesus instructing his followers about what they are required to do in time to come.

It might be helpful to compare these words with 1 Corinthians 11:23: 'For I received from the Lord that which I also delivered to you.' Here Paul records the original institution of the supper and asserts that his knowledge of it was given to him by the Lord. What he is writing provides the Corinthians with no new information. It appears that when he had first explained to the Corinthians the facts and meaning of the death of Jesus, Paul also told them about the Lord's table. His use

of the somewhat formal phrase 'that which I also delivered to
you' indicates that previous guidance about communion had
been part of the Corinthians' very early instruction in basic
Christian doctrine. Right at the beginning of their Christian
lives Paul had insisted that they gather together at the Lord's
table.

We have attempted at this point to bring the biblical
relationship between baptism and communion into focus. The
New Testament sees both as essential features of Christian
discipleship. The Head of the church ordained baptism and
included it within the terms of the commission to the apostles.
Because it was invariably practised by the New Testament
evangelists it follows that it should be considered mandatory
now. That is, churches are to be both baptized and baptizing.

Yet, given that these New Testament ordinances are to be
practised, certain questions may reverently be asked. For
example, what is the meaning of these institutions? Why is
such emphasis placed upon baptism and the Lord's table in the
Gospels, the Acts of the Apostles and the Epistles? Answers
to such questions have already been anticipated, but it may be
helpful to go into greater detail, examining baptism and the
communion meal from both doctrinal and pastoral view-
points.

4.
By water and the Word

'If you confess with your mouth the Lord Jesus and believe in your heart that God has raised him from the dead, you will be saved. For with the heart one believes to righteousness, and with the mouth confession is made to salvation' (Romans 10:9-10).

These words presuppose a fundamental phenomenon of human behaviour: that of self-expression. In the words of the Saviour himself, 'out of the abundance of the heart the mouth speaks' (Matthew 12:34).

The verses from Romans begin by stating that faith is the only instrument by which anyone can attain salvation. Conversion is an essentially personal matter, involving both an acceptance that the message of the gospel is true and a real turning to Christ. In order to be saved men and women must seek the Lord and his undeserved mercy because no action of theirs could ever merit his favour. They must rely on Christ or be lost.

Paul then says that faith which begins in the heart will be (and, indeed, must be) declared in public. He provides a reason for this sequence: 'for with the heart one believes to righteousness, and with the mouth confession is made to salvation.' This means that those who believe in Christ are to profess his name, declaring their position openly. Genuine but nevertheless undeclared faith is both an inadequate faith and perhaps an impossibility. Indeed, Christ stated that 'whoever confesses me before men, him I will also confess before my Father who is in heaven' (Matthew 10:32). In other words, it is not enough merely to admire the Lord or even to turn privately to him. To be a true disciple one must make an open confession of faith in Jesus Christ as Lord. Then, at the end, he will make an open confession to his Father that he recognises his professing disciple.

The believer's declaration

The New Testament provides baptism as the required means of declaration for the new convert. In apostolic times, whenever people came to faith in the Saviour they were baptized. There is no doubt whatever about this. Furthermore, passages which refer to specific baptisms almost always include a strong declaratory emphasis. For example, Matthew 3:6 states that many went to John the Baptist to be 'baptized by him ... confessing their sins.' Matthew 3:11 contains words from the Baptist himself to his hearers: 'I indeed baptize you with water unto repentance.' This is significant. In coming to be baptized the candidates intended to declare their repentance openly. They knew that without such a confession the process of repentance would have been incomplete. In Luke 3:7 the Baptist questions some of the crowd: 'You brood of vipers!

Who warned you to flee from the wrath to come?' He was really asking them why they had presented themselves for baptism. Apparently something had begun in their hearts which they wished to make public knowledge. Astounded at the thought that hardened Sadducees and Pharisees (Matthew 3:7) had such inclinations, he might, we suppose, have been scornfully rejecting their approach as insincere. Nevertheless, he did not query the rightness of the method.

Acts 2:38 is absolutely clear about this principle. Peter speaks to people who have come to realize that they had sinned both against God and his Son Jesus. He tells them to 'repent and be baptized': personal repentance is to be declared by water baptism, attitude being displayed and ratified by action. In later years Paul showed that he held this understanding when he referred to John's baptism: 'John indeed baptized with a baptism of repentance' (Acts 19:4). Again, while under arrest at Jerusalem the apostle mentioned his own conversion and baptism, stating that Ananias had come to him and had instructed him to 'arise and be baptized, and wash away your sins' (Acts 22:16). Paul thus understood his baptism as both an expression of sorrow for his many sins and his profession that he would now willingly forsake them. He would, as it were, wash them away.

The apostle unhesitatingly held the same understanding in connection with baptism as a symbol of new life. Water symbolizes a grave into which the repentant convert goes as one whose days as a willing sinner are now over. But he does not stay in the tomb. Almost immediately he rises up from the watery sepulchre just as his Lord vacated his own grave on the third day. In other words, Christ separated himself from a sinful, dead world, and so does the new convert: the believer leaves his old, sinful habits behind him in the grave and lives henceforth by the power of God for his Lord and Saviour.

Baptism is expounded by Paul as a magnificent and open declaration of intent.

Paul introduces this teaching because, to his intense sorrow, there were those in the Roman church who apparently knew little or nothing about personal repentance. He was compelled to ask them if they had ever realized what they were declaring when they had been baptized. The opening part of Romans 6:3 presumes, of course, that they had actually been baptized. Perhaps, he suggests, there are some at Rome who are baptized unbelievers! All in all, baptism is presented in verses 3-4 as a vividly symbolic declaration of repentance from sin and identification with Christ.

Baptism was public, vivid and initial. It was public in that the candidate was baptized: he did not so much wash himself in water as consent to be washed by another person. It was vivid because it was an outward washing. No-one who has been baptized upon profession of faith will ever forget the experience. The documents of the New Testament maintain unanimously that there was never any undue delay between conversion and baptism. New believers were not allowed to postpone their open profession. Nor, in fact, did they ever seem to wish to do so.

A profession to the believer

The New Testament speaks about another declaration made at baptism. Yes, sinners were summoned by John the Baptist, the Lord himself and then the apostles to shed their sins and turn to God. But what about those who responded? The New Testament writers state boldly and clearly that an initial assurance about the forgiveness of their sins is given to all who repent and believe in the Saviour. This declaration, moreover, is to be communicated in part by water and word together: in other words, by baptism, so reinforcing the inward testimony already granted by the Holy Spirit (Ephesians 1:13). Baptism complements initial teaching received by the convert: having come to know the peace of God he is granted a solemn declaration that he is reckoned by God to be clean.

The united teaching of John, Christ and the apostles

The basic principle of declaration from God through a human agency finds expression in the words of Christ to Peter at Caesarea Philippi: 'whatever you bind on earth will be bound in heaven, and whatever you loose on earth will be loosed in heaven' (Matthew 16:19). Peter stands here as the representative of the apostles and as such is given the 'keys of the kingdom of heaven'. He learns that his ministry in the coming days will be declarative. The Lord informs him that he will be empowered to state publicly when and under what conditions sins will or will not be forgiven. Again, just a few hours after his resurrection Jesus came to his disciples and breathed on them, saying, 'if you forgive the sins of any, they are forgiven them; if you retain the sins of any, they are retained' (John 20:23). The Lord, preparing his followers for the Day of Pentecost and for what would follow, gave them to understand that they would communicate to people the message of sins forgiven or not forgiven, according to whether or not they had turned to Christ. As his Spirit-filled representatives, the apostles would be entitled to make certain declarations about other people. Having travelled the way themselves, they could explain it to others.

This vitally important understanding permeates the later books of the New Testament. Acts portrays the band of the

apostles going out from Jerusalem to preach the good news of
the grace of God. The kernel of their message could perhaps
be summed up in Peter's words to the household of Cornelius:
'and he commanded us to preach to the people, and to testify
that it is he who was ordained by God to be Judge of the living
and the dead ... whoever believes in him will receive remission
of sins' (Acts 10:42-43). It might have been that at that
moment Peter did not anticipate the conversion of his Gentile
hearers. But it is clear that what could be termed 'pre-
conversion' evangelism was not the whole of Peter's ministry
in that home. It was when the Roman family had provided
indisputable evidence of their regeneration that the apostle
had more to say to them; he commanded them to be baptized.
In this act they both declared themselves to be believers in
Jesus and were assured that they had been accepted by the
family of faith on the ground of their acceptance by God.

This is much of the meaning of Matthew 28:19-20: 'Go
therefore and make disciples of all the nations, baptizing them
... teaching them to observe all things that I have commanded
you.' These words of Christ anticipate that the good news
would be proclaimed to all, those who received it being
baptized 'in the name of the Father and of the Son and of the
Holy Spirit'. Within this formula the word 'in' probably
means 'into': the Lord presents baptism as a means whereby
the believer is brought formally and explicitly into the fellowship of the Trinity. Thus the ordinance is a declaration from
God through the baptizer to the candidate, telling the latter that
he now belongs to the Father, the Son and the Holy Spirit and
no longer to the world. His baptism is his formal presentation
to God, whose Name is pronounced as he is washed. The
baptized believer comes away intensely aware that he is not his
own and that he has been bought with a price.

The earlier commissions from the Lord at Caesarea Philippi (Matthew 16:19) and in the upper room (John 20:23) are given form and body by the words of Matthew 28:19. The reality of the remission of the sins of the repentant sinner is stated in a vivid and personal fashion, his baptism incorporating what is effectively a two-way declaration. The convert reveals his own heart and God reveals his! Although these mutual professions are not new - at conversion the Lord will have accepted the baptismal candidate when he then turned to the Saviour - they are original in the sense that they are outward and formal. Earth makes public proclamation to heaven, and heaven to earth.

Mark 1:4 recounts the baptism commanded by John the Baptist: 'John came baptizing in the wilderness and preaching a baptism of repentance for the remission of sins.' The people whom he baptized confessed their faults in order to be forgiven. Those concerned were taught that their guilt had been cancelled, God speaking to them through the act of washing and John's accompanying words.

Peter's sermon on the Day of Pentecost again endowed baptism with this two - fold emphasis: 'repent, and let every one of you be baptized ... for the remission of sins' (Acts 2:38). Washing expresses simultaneously the sorrow of men and the mercy of God. Candidates for baptism declare that they wish to cleanse their lives, while God states that he reckons them clean in his sight.

The commitment made by the Galatians

Addressing himself to a vexed situation in the Galatian churches, Paul writes about baptism: 'for as many of you as were baptized into Christ have put on Christ' (Galatians 3:27).

The apostle is discussing justification by faith and maintains
that those who had professed Christ by being baptized in his
name had, as it were, deliberately clothed themselves in him.
By publicly identifying with the Saviour they had appropri-
ated his salvation which was now theirs. It follows that as open
expressions of their utter confidence in Christ, their baptisms
had been tantamount to formal renunciations of any prior
hopes concerning justification by works. They had 'put on'
Christ in this way because they were convinced that faith in
him would not be vain; they had really believed that he would
save to the uttermost. By baptism they entered openly and
formally into the blessings of salvation, giving themselves
unashamedly to Christ because they were assured that he
would remain their Advocate with God. Baptism had been a
prime opportunity for them to give their pledge to the Saviour
and to claim him as their own. Seeking to clothe themselves
with him, they were so clothed; they had 'put on' both Christ
and his redemption. Why then, Paul asks, did the possessors
of such declared benefits now revert to a previously - aban-
doned hope of justification by works?

The love of Christ for his church

Ephesians 5:25-27 opens up this theme still further. Paul
speaks about the Saviour who loved the church and who gave
himself for it at Calvary, suffering there for the chosen people
of God. Christ did this so that he would be able to 'sanctify'
the church and eventually present it to himself. Paul insists
that there is a cleansing action included in the whole process
of payment and acquisition, a 'washing of water by the Word'.
The sequence of thought is that Christ gave himself for his
people in order to acquire them. Having done so, he separates

them to himself by the Spirit, bringing them new life and turning them from sin. Then, the Lord himself effectively baptizes the whole church in water.

This passage does not actually include the word 'baptism', but there is no question that this is meant, the ordinance being expounded as a washing in water accompanied by words. From the practical point of view, both words and water come from the Head of the church through the agency of his servants. Although they baptize and make a certain declaration, in reality Christ is the Administrator.

This is quite remarkable teaching. Perhaps nowhere else in the New Testament's presentation of baptism does the idea of a declaration from heaven to earth come out so prominently as here. The apostle Paul, of course, is neither denying the doctrine of justification by faith nor proclaiming what might loosely be termed 'baptismal regeneration'. He teaches simply that when a convert is baptized he is being informed by the Son of God that he has been both cleansed from the guilt of sin and accepted as a member of the church. Christ himself receives him into the fellowship of his people.

Paul's reference to 'the church' in these verses makes the assumption that the whole church has been baptized in just the same way that the whole church has been ransomed: every believer will have been washed in water. Husbands, Paul advises, are to take special note. Just as Christ gave himself for all his church and has declared his love for it through baptism, so husbands are to show their love for their wives openly and obviously: certain things need to be said sometimes. Earthly husbands will please imitate the heavenly Partner! He is the model and example for heads of houses in that he delights to declare himself.

How glorious, then, is the situation of the newly-converted and baptized believer. He has been told through preaching about the grace of God towards sinners. Born again to eternal life, he has been led to believe the gospel and has been brought by the Spirit to turn to Christ for salvation. Now he knows peace with God in his heart and has been formally washed in the name of God. He has been welcomed into the family of believers by Christ himself. At baptism he has declared himself to both earth and heaven as a disciple of the Saviour. He now possesses a clear understanding that God loves him personally and has forgiven all his sins. Though limited, his spiritual experience is fresh and vigorous. He will step out with firm faith knowing that the one who bought him will never forsake him. He can only rejoice for the future.

5.
Sharing

The communion service is at the very heart and centre of
Christian worship. At the Lord's table those who believe in
Christ consider him in harmony, expressing their unity and
fellowship by eating and drinking together. Their participation in this meal proclaims both their common interest in
Christ and their involvement with each other. While it is true,
of course, that Christ saves his people individually, the idea of
sharing comes to the forefront at the Lord's table. Believers
commune together in Christ.

The situation at Corinth

This emphasis on sharing is brought out very powerfully in 1
Corinthians 10 and 11. In 10:16 Paul asks his readers a
searching question about the way in which they approach the
Lord's table. He does so in pastoral fashion, making his
opinion on the matter known and then eliciting their reply:

'The cup of blessing which we bless, is it not the communion of the blood of Christ? The bread which we break, is it not the communion of the body of Christ?' Paul's questions are basically concerned with sharing together among believers.

At Corinth there was a certain loosening of fellowship because in certain ways the people there over-emphasized their individuality. They tended to group behind favourite preachers and also showed a form of self-glorification with regard to spiritual gifts, forgetting that such gifts were given for the benefit of the whole body. It was true, of course, that they did worship together at the Lord's table in the required manner. Yet, as time wore on, the quality of worship tended to deteriorate. Gradually, some people came to consider communion as just another meal. 1 Corinthians 11:20-22 is to the point about this matter: 'When you come together in one place, it is not to eat the Lord's supper. For in eating each one takes his own supper ahead of others; and one is hungry and another is drunk. What! Do you not have houses to eat and drink in?' While Paul is obviously not denying the people their right to supply their own meals and enjoy them, he does state that when Christians come together at the Lord's table their minds should be set on more sublime matters than gastronomic pleasure. By all means let them have their full and highly-satisfying meals in their own homes, but let their fellowship meal be the 'Lord's supper'. Here every person will have an equal place and an equal portion and all will think about the Saviour.

1 Corinthians shows the Lord's table to be an ordinance for the church. Whereas baptism is experienced by believers individually, the Lord's supper is a form of worship shared by the gathered fellowship. Further reference will be made to this point, but it can be noted in passing that Paul considers communion to be the fullest possible manifestation of church

life. The problem at Corinth was that the Lord's table tended not to be a communion at all because some participants were not concerned with spiritual matters; they shared in nothing.

A message to believers

Like baptism, the Lord's table is first and foremost declarative. The words of Matthew 26:26-28 are typical of all the related accounts: 'Jesus took bread, blessed it and broke it, and gave it the the disciples and said, "Take, eat; this is my body". Then he took the cup, and gave thanks, and gave it to them, saying, "Drink from it, all of you. For this is my blood of the new covenant".' Like baptism, the communion table declares the grace of God towards sinners, encouraging and strengthening believers in their faith. It reinforces their understanding of the gospel and helps to ensure that they do not forget the price that was paid for them.

However, whereas baptism emphasizes the reality of cleansing and forgiveness, the table displays the grounds upon which God is merciful to sinners. There is in fact an obvious and deliberate development in thought from baptism to communion. The believer is given yet more to contemplate when he eats and drinks with fellow-Christians. As one who is already forgiven and who realizes that he is a child of God he is reminded in a most graphic manner that Christ died both for him and for many others, including those who commune with him.

Whereas *baptism is by tendency individualistic*, bringing new believers one by one to an initial public profession of their Lord and telling them at the same time about their happy state, the Lord's table is essentially corporate, elevating the Christian to a higher level of realization. He is given to see himself as a member of a family which has been redeemed and united under one Head. He begins to appreciate how good and pleasant it is for brethren to dwell together in unity (Psalm 133), and so he joins regularly with others who live in his own area and who have, like him, heard the good news, responded to it and professed Christ. As born-again and baptized believers they and he share the Lord's table as members of a local church.

The communion meal is thus a function and expression of Christian 'family' life. It follows that each person who wishes to participate must be known to belong to the Saviour. Unlike those worship services which are designated as 'public' and to which all people are quite rightly allowed to come, communion remains by definition restricted and private, *designed for Christian believers to the exclusion of all others.* In New Testament times Paul reacted swiftly as soon as the Corinthians showed a tendency to treat the Lord's table as an ordinary meal, just like those which they would have at home with their unconverted friends or relatives. He affirmed that the Lord's supper was not a simple meal for anyone who chose to be present; it was an occasion for the sharing of a common faith.

6.
Remembrance

When the Lord's people meet at his table they set their minds upon the historic fact of Calvary. The fellowship meal was intended by Christ to bring to the remembrance of participants the reality and meaning of his death, strengthening the ties between the Saviour and the saved. The contemplation of the symbols of his suffering would bring blessing and encouragement to the soul by recalling exactly why he died. The Lord meant his table to take believing people back to the cross.

'This do', he commanded, 'in remembrance of me' (1 Corinthians 11:25). At communion believers consider the death of Christ because he himself is the centre of their worshipful thought and attention. The table was ordained so that those around it might consider Jesus and not just the events of the crucifixion. The whole thrust of Christ's teaching concerns that personal relationship which exists between Christians and their Lord.

The new covenant displayed

In presenting the bread and the wine to his disciples at the Last

Supper the Lord said, 'This is my body which is broken for you ... This cup is the new covenant in my blood' (1 Corinthians 11:24-25). Poured-out wine brings to mind his violent death because it represents his shed blood, spilt to seal what he described as a 'new' covenant.

At this final meal with his followers before he died Jesus gave an explanation of his imminent sufferings. He anticipated that his blood would ratify a covenant between God and those whom he proposed to serve as their sacrificing Priest. Set in the context of a Passover meal, the Lord's words compare and contrast this 'new' covenant with the old covenant inaugurated by Moses at Sinai. Jesus indicated that although the new would be similar in some respects to the old, it would be a significant improvement. 'New' was only another way of saying 'better'; the old was about to become obsolete.

Old Testament predictions

In speaking about the blood of a 'new covenant' the Lord was referring his hearers to two chapters in the Old Testament: Exodus 24 and Jeremiah 31. In days long since gone, God covenanted with his people Israel whom he had then recently delivered from Egypt. He consented to be their God and continuing benefactor if they for their part would honour his laws. When they openly agreed to do so Moses took sacrificial blood and sprinkled it upon the people, thereby sealing the covenant. The record of Scripture states that 'he took the book of the covenant and read in the hearing of the people. And they said "All that the Lord has said we will do, and be obedient." And Moses took the blood, sprinkled it on the people, and said,

"Behold, the blood of the covenant which the Lord has made with you according to all these words" ' (Exodus 24:7-8).

Moses knew that this covenant would be broken continually by the people. Furthermore, he knew why: their hearts were basically sinful and the great majority of them would never know the fear of the Lord nor learn to love him. The prophet was unhappily aware that their fervent promises could and would not stand the test of time. Later history was to confirm his worst fears: over the centuries Israel habitually neglected the God of their fathers. The eventual consequence was that in time God severed the relationship which he had confirmed with his people at Sinai; Israel was evicted from the promised land.

Yet the breakdown of this old covenant was not the end of God's dealings with the family of Abraham. Just at the time when Judah was to be removed by military action from the homeland the prophet would predict a 'new' covenant with his people. The old covenant, now hopelessly shattered, had never provided any basis for a lasting relationship between God and the people and would never be renewed by the Lord. However, a 'new' covenant would be reached, far superior in every way, a covenant in which those who pledged themselves to serve God would have been redeemed from an adversary far more fearful than Pharoah in the time of Moses. Moreover, those whom God was to save would not only make their vows sincerely but would be given the power to keep them: the Lord himself would see to it that within the framework of this new and better arrangement there would be provision from him to establish the lasting faithfulness of his people; he would keep them from falling and see to it that none would ever be allowed to forsake him.

A further difference between the two covenants would be the wider scope of the second. Not confining itself to one race, it would include people from every part of the world. This, however, is not mentioned by Jeremiah, who is more concerned to expound the quality of the new covenant than its enlarged constituency. Accordingly, his prophecy includes the following remarkable statement: 'Behold, the days are coming... when I will make a new covenant... not according to the covenant that I made with their fathers ... I will put my law in their minds, and write it on their hearts; and I will be their God, and they shall be my people' (31:31-33).

Although the prophet does not speak here about the necessary legal basis for this covenant because he is concerned with the subjective aspect alone, other Old Testament writers do. In just the same way as blood was shed to ratify the old covenant, in the new-covenant situation a sacrifice would be made to justify the people before their holy God. Because no Levitical priest could possibly render a true and sufficient propitiation for the sins of his fellows the Old Testament anticipates that God himself will graciously provide a priest to offer himself. Furthermore, it is predicted that this sacrifice will be followed by the renewal of the hearts of the intended beneficiaries who will always wish to remain within the covenant. For this reason this covenant will be perpetually fresh and never outmoded. The priest, of course, eventually came: Jesus, from Nazareth in Galilee.

The security of the believer

At the Lord's table, therefore, the spiritually-renewed people of God look back and remember their Lord in the days of his flesh. They contemplate the historic fact of Calvary, reminding themselves that the sufferings of Christ constitute the judicial basis for their peaceful standing with God. They reflect that because Jesus offered perfect obedience to his

Father he was raised from the dead and was given the promised Holy Spirit whom, they know, he has now sent to them. They realise that because they have been born again to eternal life they will never cease to love and serve their God. The bread and wine speak to them about the perfect sacrificial basis of this new and eternal covenant which, unlike the old, remains invulnerable. The people of God will never contract out of it because God in three Persons has established them in it. When they are together at the Lord's table Christian people rejoice in their Redeemer who has given them absolute security.

7.
Family life

Paul's teaching about communion in 1 Corinthians 11:23-26 concerns church life as well as history. He writes not only about the fact of Calvary and its meaning but also about the continual appreciation of that which Christ achieved, reproducing the words of the Lord himself: 'Take, eat ... do this in remembrance... this do, as often as you drink it, in remembrance of me'. The apostle then gives his own inspired comment about what believers actually do at the Lord's table: 'For as often as you eat this bread and drink this cup, you proclaim the Lord's death till he comes'. The passage emphasizes that communion is no ordinary meal, the pointed reference to 'this' bread and 'this' cup indicating that the purpose for which Christian people come together is aided by bread and wine, the Lord's table being a meal by which the death of Christ is declared. The meal is not in any way a convivial occasion.

The symbolism of bread and wine

At communion believers renew their relationship with the Lord Jesus Christ. Bread and wine are provided in nominal amounts, but nevertheless constitute a meal. Worshippers take bread and eat it and receive wine and drink it. The essential diference between this provision and an ordinary meal is that 'this' bread and 'this' wine represent the body and blood of the Saviour. The people consume emblems of Christ crucified, becoming symbolically united with him. Their action reflects their desire to remain spiritually united with the Lord. In communion together they determine to come to him and receive him.

There is no question, of course, that this bread and wine remain only bread and wine, even though they have been deliberately set aside to portray the crucified Saviour. When the communicant worshipper eats and drinks these symbols he is, or should be, engaging in worship. He will, by the exercise of faith, receive Christ into his soul even as he did when he was originally converted. The bread and wine help him to do this because they are symbols which vividly illustrate the Saviour who died for him personally. Summoned by the Lord himself, the believer meditates upon Christ. He understands quite clearly that the bread and wine are not Christ and do not 'contain' the Lord in any sacramental form. Nevertheless, the believer's consumption of the meal is an act of worship in which he is engaged in direct prayer to the Redeemer. His senses influenced by the bread and wine, he prays that the Saviour may dwell with him even as these appointed symbols become an integral part of his bodily system.

A source of misunderstanding

The Lord's table will be of immense benefit to the believer if
he understands it properly. It presents to him the blessings of
the gospel. Yet it is not difficult to imagine that the memorial
meal could easily be abused. Suppose, for example, that an
unconverted person is present at communion. Because he has
no prior experience of personal faith in Christ he will not
understand the pure symbolism of the bread and wine nor the
deeply spiritual motives which brings others to worship in this
way. For him the whole service will be only an external rite.
He might even think that the elements are Christ. If this should
be so, reasoning might bring him to the conclusion that the
mere act of eating and drinking will actually bring God to him.

Clearly, it is absolutely necessary that those who come to
the Lord's table must be born again by the Spirit to believe in
Christ for their salvation. Moreover, it is essential that they
should have declared their faith before the Lord's people,
having given some prior demonstration that they are children
of God. If this condition is not met there is the possibility that
the intensely spiritual meaning of communion will be ob-
scured, the Lord's table being to a greater or lesser extent
misunderstood and misapplied.

Casual Christians

In coming to the communion table the believer obviously joins
with other Christians. It follows that if this act of worship
deepens the Christian's relationship with his Saviour it will
also strengthen his bonds with his fellow worshippers. In fact,
'communion' refers primarily to relationships between

Christians and not to the union which exists between the believer and Christ.

This is brought out powerfully by Paul's admonitions to the Corinthians. As we have observed, 1 Corinthians 11:20-22 reveals that some people in that church were progressively reducing the Lord's table to the status of an ordinary meal. The symbolism of bread and wine was largely discounted and too little attention was given to fellowship; people were coming along merely to eat and drink and indulge in conversation; no higher purpose was involved. Because Paul considered this to be wrong and unworthy, he exhorted the Corinthians to give careful consideration to the original meaning of the Lord's supper before they actually attended it. They were instructed to give thought to the words of the one who instituted the meal and also to their fellow-participants. The prospective worshipper was to examine himself in the light of all that the table of the Lord stood for. He was to consider his motives because a casual attitude would detract from the quality of fellowship required. Paul therefore continues: 'Let a man examine himself, and so let him eat of that bread and drink of that cup. For he who eats and drinks in an unworthy manner eats and drinks judgement to himself, not discerning the Lord's body' (1 Corinthians 11:28-29). The 'Lord's body' here almost certainly means Christian people in communion: Christ is in them but not in the symbols, which only represent him. The presence of the Lord is discerned by the sensitive participant to be among the people seated happily together. Paul's point is that he who does not give this fact adequate thought but nevertheless presents himself at the table must render a deep disservice to all concerned. Failing to appreciate that the table represents the Lord and that the people, as it were, contain the Saviour, he will not discern the intense spirituality of the meal and will spoil the harmony of the occasion, introducing an element of discord. In fact, he will bring a judgement upon himself.

The maintenance of basic discipline

God's judgement was actually present at Corinth. Yet even those whose motivation Paul deemed unworthy were professing and baptized Christians; there is absolutely no evidence to the contrary. What effect, therefore, might there have been upon fellowship and worship if there had come to the Lord's table in the Corinthian church people who had never made an open profession of faith in Christ, who had never been baptized and who did not really belong to that or to any other fellowship of Christian people? It is to be presumed, of course, that this never happened; the apostle only inveighs against those who are apparently within the fellowship. The idea of unbelievers attending communion does not appear to arise.

The declaring church

1 Corinthians 11:26 clearly emphasizes the necessity of spiritual discernment on the part of the worshippers at communion: 'For as often as you eat this bread and drink this cup, you proclaim the Lord's death till he comes'. Paul knew that if the Lord's table is to fulfil the purpose for which it was instituted it must be allowed to attract to itself spiritually-minded people alone. The bread, of course, represents the body of the Lord and the wine his blood, while the actual breaking of bread and pouring of wine are deeply symbolic. Nevertheless, it is the actual consumption of these elements which declares the

atonement wrought by Christ. When the people eat and drink they themselves, and not the emblems, are the exhibitors. This means that there is far more to communion than the contemplation of the bread and wine as symbols; actual eating and drinking in fellowship by Christians who know and love the Lord is the means by which Calvary is portrayed. So, says Paul, when believers at Corinth eat and drink they show forth personally the death of Christ: 'you proclaim the Lord's death'.

What an amazing statement! The apostle declares in effect that the emblems by themselves cannot possibly make a sufficient declaration of the death of the Messiah even though they were instituted by the Saviour himself. The bread and wine need people if they are to fulfil their function. Moreover, they require people of a particular type: regenerated believers. Then, when Christians come to the table of the Lord to worship their God in harmony together there is a definite consequence: they 'proclaim the Lord's death', declaring a Saviour who died for them and who has actually brought them to his Father.

This 'family' aspect of communion could be illustrated by contrasting a house with a home: a house is only a building whereas a home is a building with people in it, people who live together as one family. Their house will be filled with light, warmth, affection, joys, sadness, caring and growth, in fact, all the ingredients of family life. So it should be, implies Paul, with the church especially when it meets at the Lord's table. The table is only furniture, and while the bread and wine may have a special purpose they can never be anything more than they are. However, when the Christian family shares its life together at communion the purpose of the table is fulfilled.

A building might be grand in its construction and might even be filled with expensive furniture. Yet without caring people within its walls it would simply not be a home. Similarly, the Lord's table speaks about infinite cost, its fare declaring an expensive sacrifice, the Christ who died. Yet it is only when the family comes together at the communion table in love and unity that his death is seen for what it was, an effective sacrifice made to bring men unfailingly to God and to each other. A table surrounded by worshipful, loving, sharing, God-fearing, remembering, giving, caring people is a table put to good use. Believers, together with bread and wine, join to announce that Christ has died and that his death has accomplished its purpose. This alone, says Paul, is communion. The table by itself or with undiscerning people in attendance says nothing that is helpful or worthwhile. For this reason the Corinthians are exhorted to ensure that no one comes to their communion who does not have his mind set on heavenly things.

Everywhere in his discussion the apostle assumes that worshippers at the supper are professing believers and, as such, have been baptized. This inference follows from the fact that the baptismal teaching of 1 Corinthians 10:1-2 precedes Paul's whole treatment of communion. He entertains the fervent hope that the people will have developed healthy spiritual appetites and will leave their bodily desires at home when they come to the fellowship meal in order to remember Christ together. They all need to discern the tremendous gulf between the world and the church of God and must desire to set their hearts on things unseen. Paul teaches clearly that any obscuring of such standards would inevitably give an undue emphasis to the outward. If this should be the case the motions of worship will be to a greater or lesser extent lifeless and mechanical. With people of reduced spirituality the triumph of Calvary must be proportionately concealed. In fact, the impression could be given, albeit unintentionally, that the death of Christ had achieved little for the people gathered together. Their negative behaviour would prove that they have nothing worthwhile to declare.

8.
Anticipation

As the focus of the life and fellowship of the local church, the Lord's table points worshippers to the secure future of the people of God as a whole. Christ took the Jewish Passover and adapted it as a meal in memory of those sufferings which he would shortly undergo and as an anticipation of the glory to be revealed at the end of the world. At the Last Supper he showed his awareness that he would remain the Head of a church which would continue until the end of time and then in eternity: 'But I say to you, I will not drink of this fruit of the vine from now until that day when I drink it new with you in my Father's kingdom' (Matthew 26:29).

In thus addressing the apostles the Lord was anticipating not only his death but also his resurrection, ascension, heavenly session as the Priest of his church and final advent. Moreover, he was quite sure that he would live to drink wine again at a specified time to which he referred as 'that day', the last of all days when he would appear again to judge the world. He asserted that the wine to be drunk on that occasion with his disciples would be 'new', entirely fresh wine, indicative of a new phase or state of being for the kingdom of God. Indeed, he would drink on that day in his Father's kingdom rather than his own, implying that then his work would be entirely complete (1 Corinthians 15:24,28). Only when his sufferings, his heavenly ministry, his final return and his activity as the judge of all are accomplished would he drink. On the night when he was betrayed the Saviour spoke, ate and drank in truly prophetic fashion, looking ahead to the consummation of redemption.

The apostle Paul insists that the same elements of glorious certainty are present whenever a church meets at the Lord's table: 'For as often as you eat this bread, and drink this cup, you proclaim the Lord's death till he comes' (1 Corinthians 11:26). Obviously, Paul did not believe that the first readers of the Corinthian letter would remain alive until the Lord returned. He was deliberately speaking not only to the Corinthian and other believers in their generation but to the Lord's people of all times and nations, implying that new converts will see later converts, evangelism continuing to the end of time. Paul is prophetic in this verse, visualising the church of God persevering and continually expanding. He sees the people of God in different places and centuries gathering at tables to eat and drink in holy fellowship. 'Whenever you do this', he says 'you will show forth the death of Christ. And you will be doing this until the very day that he comes again.'

What magnificent teaching! At the Lord's table believers remember the great, historic sacrifice rendered to God for the satisfaction of their sins. They know that down through the ages there have already been many who so worshipped. They are aware that in their own age there are many Christian churches around the world which gather according to Christ's Word. Furthermore, they take to their hearts the knowledge that the church of Christ can never fail to persevere as the years go by. What has been will be because when the current generation of believers has gone others will follow. There will always be conversions, baptisms, churches and communion tables with glad believers around them. It must always be so until that day when Christ shall come again. Then, the wine will be 'new'.

At the Lord's table, then, Christians rejoice and lift up their heads because the day of their full redemption approaches. They worship in the confidence that all for whom he died must come to Christ and that when he returns the crucified and risen Saviour will be entirely satisfied with his work. At his table churches praise God in anticipation of that which shall be.

9.
Coming together

To repeat a point made in previous pages, Paul's first letter to
the Corinthians shows clearly that the communion meal was
the heart and soul of New Testament church life. Furthermore,
1 Corinthians, more than all the other correspondence in the
New Testament, deals with various ills and problems which
can so easily arise in a local fellowship.

This observation is important because it emphasizes the
practical context of the Lord's table. Although the Saviour's
institution of the memorial meal is found in the Gospel accounts, the way in which the early Christians interpreted
communion is shown by chapters 10 and 11 of this letter.
These chapters give the obvious impression that Paul recognized that they were observing the ordinance as a 'church'
institution. That is, the people clearly considered communion
as an occasion, perhaps the occasion, for their church to meet
together.

In Paul's day the Lord's table was recognized as the focus
of association and worship for members of a church. It was not
really thought about as a meeting-point for believers coming

Chustians comming together

together from churches in the surrounding vicinity; the apostle simply does not discuss communion as an occasion for inter-church fellowship. Doubtless, such a usage might have been perfectly feasible within a limited area in which various fellowships could have met at an agreed venue. That this pattern nowhere appears in the New Testament is due un-doubtedly to the emphasis which Scripture places upon the congregational order of the churches. Because the independent fellowship, endowed with the Spirit, is a microcosm of the whole church, there is no necessity whatever to extract the Lord's table from such a setting. To do so, however inno-cently, would erode the concept of the autonomy of the local church. The New Testament realizes this.

The treatment of the matter given in 1 Corinthians is comprehensive, the epistle assuming that what Paul both approved and required at Corinth was normative in all the churches of his time (1 Corinthians 11:16). Therefore it is to be so now. The apostle sees communion as a basic form of worship for Christians who normally come together on a regular basis. Again, because there is no unit smaller or larger than that of the gathered church in the New Testament econ-omy, it follows that the Lord's table is essentially a powerful expression of assembly life.

This understanding is strongly reinforced by the repeated use of the words 'come together', which appear no less than seven times in 1 Corinthians. The concentration in usage is significant, especially when it is considered that five of these occurences are in chapter 11 and are within the context of teaching about the Lord's table. The seven references are 11:17, 11:18, 11:20, 11:33, 11:34, 14:23 and 14:26.

11:17: 'I do not praise you, since you come together not for the better but for the worse.' Paul knew, of course, that the

Corinthians met because they had long since developed a formal pattern of church life. Although this claimed his unreserved blessing he did not at all approve of what frequently occurred when the people gathered. The way in which they did this caused him distress.

11:18: 'For first of all, when you come together as a church, I hear that there are divisions.' Paul is now more explicit, knowing that the Corinthians meet as a 'church'. Their gatherings are deliberate and include a certain degree of formality. This is acknowledged by a suffix to the words 'come together'; they do so as a 'church'.

11:20: 'When you come together' expands verses 17 and 18. The association which the Corinthians enjoyed was essentially local. Paul is quite explicit about the context in which he knows they set the Lord's table. The believers all agree to meet together at a mutually-acceptable venue where they would remember the Lord in the appointed manner. The pity of it was that the attitudes of the various worshippers tended to empty their communion of much of its meaning. Nevertheless, the idea of coming together in one place was well entrenched and quite proper.

11:33: 'Therefore, my brethren, when you come together to eat, wait for one another.' The principle of setting the Lord's supper squarely within a local-church background is again clearly presented here. Paul understands that there are those times when the Corinthian fellowship gathers together for the express purpose of eating and drinking at the Lord's table: this is their whole agenda. The point is made here that if communion is meant for the church, it is meant for all the church: let everyone be in communion. No one is to remain aloof or, on the other hand, feel unwanted.

11:34: 'But if anyone is hungry, let him eat at home, lest you come together for judgement.' The words 'come together' are repeated to emphasize the idea of Christians belonging together in their church. The Lord's table must never be considered as an opportunity for satisfying natural hunger: believers should return to their homes if they want a good meal. At communion the elements will be present in nominal amounts and for symbolic purposes only.

14:23 and 26: 'If the whole church comes together in one place' and 'whenever you come together'. These two verses are concerned with aspects of church life other than communion but, nevertheless, proclaim locality. They presuppose the principle of the gathered church, there being those occasions when all the people join together at one place for the sole purpose of worship.

In commending this principle Paul is entirely consistent with all that the New Testament has to say elsewhere about the organizing of visible churches. Gospels, Acts and Epistles all subscribe to this 'cellular' concept, representing each company of believers as a complete and fully-developed unit. The unit relates, of course, to other cells, but if need be it will be able to persevere by itself. The New Testament emphasizes that within the cell should be found all the various components which define the body of the Christ who dwells within it, giving life to the whole fellowship even as he has granted life to each believer.

It is not unreasonable to believe that this stress upon the communion of the saints in a local setting is suited ideally to the needs and talents of the people concerned. Although independence can only enhance inter-dependence (individual cells always being inter-related), it avoids cumbersome and impersonal inter-church bureaucracy with its attendant dangers. In their various churches Christians will realize that they have a real place in the life of that body of Christ to which they belong. They will feel that together they are significant, a focus for the work of the Holy Spirit in ministry and outreach. Given its life from the Lord, the gathered communion of baptized believers will pursue its worship and fellowship. While it should always appreciate other churches and involve itself with them as opportunities and needs arise it will seek to work out its own destiny, its people being those who at all times 'come together'.

10.
The local church: an Old Testament example

1 Corinthians 10:1-11 compares Christian believers in their churches to the children of Israel at the time of the exodus. Christ, declares Paul, was with Moses and his people all the way from the Red Sea to Canaan one and a half millennia before the Lord by the Spirit came to Corinth (cf. Ephesians 2:17). Further, like the Corinthians, Moses and the children of Israel were both baptized and ate and drank from a table provided by the Lord. Paul's point is that because of these direct parallels lessons are to be drawn from the experience of an ancient people.

Israel, a gathered church

In drawing an analogy between Israel in the exodus and the experience of Christian people Paul concerns himself in 1 Corinthians with a discussion of Christian behaviour. The strength of the parallel is that the Israelites, freshly redeemed from bondage, underwent a form of baptism, became a united and organized fellowship, and enjoyed a provision supplied them by the Saviour himself. They ate and drank, as it were, from a table in the wilderness in which they were effectively a 'congregation' (Acts 7:38; AV 'church'). Unhappily, the vast majority of those who left Egypt never reached Canaan. Despite the fact that they had seen the power of God at work in the land of the Pharaohs and had passed through the waters of the Red Sea to follow Moses into the wilderness, most of that first generation died there. The reason for their tragic end was that their religion was entirely superficial: the love of God had never been in them. For this reason the Lord declined to retain them: 'but with most of them God was not well pleased, for their bodies were scattered in the wilderness' (1 Corinthians 10:5); their failure to reach Canaan proved conclusively that they had incurred the displeasure of the Lord. Yet this tragedy serves to strengthen rather than weaken the force of the illustration. A later church, that at Corinth, was required to learn from the failures of an earlier gathered fellowship, that of Israel in Sinai.

Israel, a baptized church

In stating that these Israelites had been 'baptized', Paul refers his readers to Exodus 14:19-22. At the Red Sea the cloud of the divine presence took station between Israel and the Egyptian enemy and the waters divided on either side of Moses and his people. In effect the Hebrews were given only one direction in which to move: eastward, out of Egypt and towards the land from which their fathers had come. They were being led from the furnace of Egypt into a life of pilgrimage and faith in their God, their exit becoming a type of baptistery. Hedged in on three sides, north, south and west, by water and cloud, they moved eastward to commence a completely new pattern of life under the leadership of Moses. They 'all were baptized into Moses in the cloud and in the sea' (1 Corinthians 10:2), becoming a coherent and quite separate body of people, distinct from the surrounding idolatrous world. As such, they were provided by the Lord with manna and water until they arrived at the land of promise.

Israel, a separate church

In this exposition the apostle proclaims in effect that baptism in water is the obvious distinctive dividing the church from the world. Because the baptismal experience of Israel was analogous to that of all the Corinthians, the latter could learn much from their 'fathers'. Like them, they too had passed through water at the very beginning of their pilgrimage to sit at a special table provided by the Lord himself. They too were constituted a distinct communion.

It is noteworthy that although most of the Corinthian believers would have been Greek by birth, Paul addresses them as if they were Israelites; they were no longer 'Gentiles': 'But I say that the things which the Gentiles sacrifice they sacrifice to demons and not to God, and I do not want you to have fellowship with demons' (1 Corinthians 10:20). The lesson here is that Israel of old had compromised itself seriously in spite of the fact of deliverance from Egypt. Although they had been given a new life, baptism, a table and a promise for the future, most of the people perished in the desert because they had offended God. The Corinthians, surrounded as they were by pagan uncleanness, were to take note and were not to fall into sin as did those whom Paul terms 'all our fathers'.

At the exodus the people of Israel 'were all baptized', verse 2, and 'all ate the same spiritual food, and all drank the same spiritual drink', verses 3-4. Everyone who came out of Egypt passed through water. This happened to them as a matter of course and, indeed, could not have been avoided: any who had not passed through the Red Sea would obviously not have remained among Moses' travelling people. Paul implies that this was a shadow or type of discipleship in the Messianic dispensation. Similarly, those redeemed by the Saviour are to be baptized upon profession of faith with a view to sharing fellowship at the Lord's table. In fact, the analogy provided by Israel almost suggests a necessity laid upon the believer in Christ: what was essential for Israel is no less so for members of the church.

Whatever the apostle's complaints about the Corinthians, he does not criticize any of the people because they have not been baptized or because they absent themselves from the Lord's supper. In these respects there is no failure: all concerned have been involved properly in the externals of the faith. His lament is that the people display a distinct tendency to contradict their holy calling, just as Israel did, and that even when they did come to communion some bring the atmosphere of the world with them. Their attitude was unhealthy even though the framework in which they met was basically sound.

At every point in his discourse Paul presents baptism and the remembrance meal as hallmarks of a Christian church. The analogy with the Corinthian situation is in no way weakened by the fact that most of the baptized and communicant members of the church of Israel were obviously unregenerate. Because they had been redeemed, immersed upon a profession of trust in Moses' leadership and fed from heaven the Israelites should never have displeased God in the ways that they did. Similarly, because they regularly communed at the Lord's table as baptized members of their church, the Corinthians had to guard against the temptations of a world just as sinful as it had been in Moses' day.

The urgent call to holiness sounded by this chapter would not be nearly so insistent if it did not presume the redemption and baptism of all who attended communion. Israel had absolutely no excuse whatever for sin. Nor have Christians, whose participation at the remembrance meal makes any lapse all the more shocking.

11.
The wisdom of Scripture

'Let all things be done decently and in order' (1 Corinthians
14:40). Although this remark falls outside Paul's discussion
of the ordinances it is relevant because it concerns 'all things'.
Everything that occurs within the fellowship of the church
should be characterized by reverence and orderly procedure.
If not, God will be dishonoured and the people injured.

It is a truism that the New Testament prescribes baptism
for all disciples when they first profess the faith. So is the
observation that in the earliest days Christians joined together
in organized fellowships both to meet at communion and
generally to pursue their high calling as the people of God. It
is the thesis of these pages that the New Testament pattern
should continue to be applied precisely. Contemporary
churchmanship should be exact. Yet not all would agree with
this position.

Ambiguity

It seems that more often than not the practical administration
of the Lord's table in the churches today tends to overlook
much which, according to the exposition presented here,
Scripture deems necessary. For example, baptism following
a profession of faith is not always required of those who are
invited to attend communion services observed immediately
after morning or evening worship. Often, all believers are
invited openly to participate. Occasionally there is no invitation at all. In such cases, although the Lord's table is seen to
be prepared and it is obvious that there must be those who
propose to meet there, terms of welcome or admission are not
stated. Any visitors who happen to be present remain unaware
of the local procedure unless they ask somebody.

   On the other hand, it is not unknown for churches to be
accused of a certain lack of Christian charity if they only invite
to their communion visiting baptized believers who might be
present. It has been claimed naively that the table belongs to
the Lord and not to the church. Who, then, are ministers and
officers that they deny the emblems of bread and wine to some
of the Lord's dear people? Surely all believers possess the
right to attend a communion service if they so wish? Differ-
ences in baptismal practice, it is sometimes urgently proclaimed, should not be allowed to lead to division at the Lord's
table. Tolerance in matters which are not essential for salvation must be the order of the day in view of the fact that there
are so many humble and knowledgeable Christian people
who, for reasons which they consider quite sufficient, have
never been immersed upon profession of faith. Thus, it is
alleged, it is quite wrong to make a particular form of baptism
a condition for communicant worship. Churches which insist
that the Lord's table is the proper expression of the life of the

local fellowship of baptized believers and insist that visitors may attend only if they submit to the prevailing discipline tend to attract criticism.

The more tolerant view in its various forms is so pervasive and (let it be admitted) so persuasive that it has to be considered carefully and not unsympathetically. Upon closer examination, however, it shows itself to be defective and counter-productive.

The authority of Christ

The Saviour instructed the eleven to baptize, that is, to immerse, all converts (Matthew 28:19) and it is clear that the apostles took the Lord's command seriously. The New Testament, in fact, says nothing about unbaptized believers or, indeed, the baptism of any save professing believers. If baptism ceases to be a necessary prerequisite for communion, confessedly the focus of all Christian fellowship, then the churches concerned are to some extent disobedient and in confrontation with their Head.

Pastoral responsibility

Baptism was ordained by Christ for the benefit of individual believers. It follows that if an eldership does not insist that all who come to the Lord's table (transient visitors included) be immersed in the New Testament manner, it is acting against the interests of the people by implying that an ordained means of grace is to be to some extent devalued: unbaptized believers are led, albeit in a somewhat indirect manner and no doubt quite unintentionally, into a form of disobedience.

Confession

Baptism is essentially declarative in function and, as such, meets certain basic emotional and spiritual needs. Like the man born blind but given his sight by the Saviour (John 9), true faith in Christ will be ready and willing to speak for itself. Open profession is an intensely satisfying matter. The Lord instituted baptism so that his people could express themselves properly.

To downgrade baptism to the level of a highly desirable but nevertheless non-essential feature of church life is to cast doubt upon the value of a means by which believers can consolidate their faith by professing Christ as Saviour and Lord. Again, this form of relaxation is pastorally unsatisfactory because it is contrary to the interests of the people.

The assurance of salvation

Baptism expresses simultaneously the repentance and faith of the newly born-again believer and the grace of God to him. Water was administered by the apostles as the sign of the remission of sins. In a personal and notably vivid fashion converts were given to understand that their sins had been cleansed away through faith in Christ, an understanding which they needed in a hostile and sinful world.

If baptism comes to be regarded as optional for believers (and this is the attitude necessarily adopted in practice by any form of 'open' communion) there will be some degree of interference with an ordained channel of communication between heaven and earth. Clearly, this is a most serious matter, tending possibly towards uncertainty about salvation.

For example, a young unbaptized Christian, deprived of this external help through lack of responsible leadership in his church, would have to rely solely on his meagre understanding of the Bible, his very immature spiritual experience and his limited appreciation of Christian fellowship as he begins his pilgrimage. Nor would an older unbaptized believer necessarily be in any better position.

Confusion in the church

Furthermore, any relaxation of this basic New Testament procedure would allow the distinct possibility of unconverted people attending the communion table. No doubt there are those who confess Christ as Lord at their baptism without knowing him as such. Sadly, there are many Baptist churches which neither hold nor proclaim evangelical doctrine. Yet, arguably, non-Baptist churches are far more guilty in this respect. A church's welcome to the Lord's table to all who consider that they believe in the Lord Jesus Christ without requiring their baptism upon an explicit profession of faith is not greatly different from opening communion to the world at large. It is a sad fact that since the age of the apostles opinions have differed remarkably as to the essentials of the Christian faith. Is it unreasonable, therefore, to expect that a local church should apply certain practical standards to the matter of communion, that is, the standards prescribed by the New Testament? This is especially necessary in a nominally Christian but actually pagan society such as ours.

The apostle complained that 'when you come together in one place, it is not to eat the Lord's supper' (1 Corinthians 11:20). His readers were professing Christians, had been baptized and were in the happy custom of joining at a fellowship meal. Nevertheless, their attitudes and practices at communion were such that, whatever it might have been in its inception, the meal was certainly not the Lord's table in reality.

A communion meal to which all and sundry are in effect (although perhaps not intentionally) invited will look like the Lord's table but might not be so in fact. The validity of a remembrance meal does not rest in the display of bread and wine nor solely in an orthodox and acceptable background theology for the ordinance. 'Communion' is concerned with a basic relationship between those who actually attend: if unity in spiritual matters is not present and if Christian love is absent, the meal might remain only a meal. The practice of 'open' communion runs this particular risk far more than communion to which baptized believers alone are invited.

12.
Transient communion

What response is to be shown by a baptized church when a Christian who has not been immersed upon profession of faith seeks to worship at its communion? It is obvious to most Baptist pastors and churches that this situation is not infrequent. The issue becomes complicated when, as sometimes happens, it is clear that the visiting non-Baptist is a knowledgeable and sincere believer who genuinely wishes to share fellowship inoffensively with his Baptist friends in their church. In such a case any failure by the host church to give its visitor a genuine welcome could well be embarrassing and hurtful unless Christian grace and wisdom are shown by all concerned.

The only way to deal adequately with this question of transient communion is to arrive at a conclusion based on New Testament principles. It has been the task of these pages to try to demonstrate what these are. Their application might well be as follows:

Any local fellowship of Christians which identifies itself as a 'church' should, as a matter of principle, be baptized and baptize, that is, immerse, all whom it receives to its communion.

Furthermore, visitors who wish to participate at the Lord's table should expect and be expected to comply with the discipline and procedure pertaining in the fellowship, even though they may come from a different tradition. This is to some extent a matter of courtesy and etiquette although, at heart, it is a doctrinal issue.

This means that transient visitors must be baptized upon profession of faith already if they wish to attend communion.

Although this discipline seems rigorous, it may be said to be in the interests of:

Unbaptized visiting believers who need teaching and pastoral guidance in this matter, notwithstanding their possible disagreement with such a position.

The host fellowship, which can only be helped by a consistent attitude shown without exception towards all believers.

The local pastoral ministry, which is required by Scripture to baptize all disciples who place themselves under its influence. The reception of visiting unbaptized believers into communion is tantamount to a failure to discharge a basic pastoral duty.

General influence: like any school, a local church will only be seen to care properly when it provides both sound teaching and sensible discipline. The humble maintenance of what is reasoned to be a New Testament procedure might well gain the respect of other people, transient visitors and unbaptized Christians not excluded.

Consistency: either baptism upon profession of faith is a necessary qualification for attendance at the Lord's table or it is not. If it is, exceptions should never be made. If it is not, it should never appear in any invitation to a communion in which all believers must have a right to share. Any middle way must lack conviction and be dissatisfying.

Conclusion

The point is sometimes made that even those churches which only welcome to their communion accredited, that is, baptized, believers nevertheless fail to show impressive signs of spiritual growth. This might be a fair criticism of some fellowships, it is to be admitted. Yet we might remember that although the Corinthian communion included those alone who had been baptized as believers its many tensions did not originate with this procedure. On the contrary, the latter was a necessary check without which total chaos would undoubtedly have supervened.

Forms of administration by themselves never guarantee spiritual life. Yet they are essential. While the church which prides itself on being orthodox in the ordering of its ways might ultimately come to a sad state, the fellowship which relaxes the New Testament norm could well find itself in greater difficulties in the longer term. An under-emphasis on distinctives is no improvement upon an exact presentation.

Within the fellowship of the local church there has to be much more than loyalty to accepted procedures. There needs to be Christian love and compassion, sharing and sympathy. Believers must know how to weep for one another and rejoice with each other. The Word of God must be proclaimed graciously and truthfully. Of course, unenlightened 'orthodoxy', where, or indeed if, it exists, must be dreadfully uninteresting. In fact, it would be fatal to the growth of the church so afflicted. Yet unorthodoxy is far, far worse.

Postscript

To return to the beakers and the knives: it is quite possible to construct a platform for a fourth beaker.

Place the handles of the three knives on top of the upturned beakers, with the blades pointing towards each other. Interlock the ends of the blades (if you try this, you will discover what is meant). The knives will offer mutual support, providing sufficient area for a platform. Take any one away and the other two will collapse.

Baptism, the local church and the Lord's table are intimately locked together in the teaching of the New Testament. United, the three form a foundation upon which the Christian can build his spiritual life. Separated, they lose much of their individual significance. It is submitted that herein lies the scriptural testimony to the wisdom and practice of restricted communion.